EASY PIANO

BEST OF CARPENTERS

I0812145

ISBN 978-0-634-03236-3

HAL•LEONARD® CORPORATION

7777 W. BLUEMOUND RD. P.O. BOX 13819 MILWAUKEE, WI 53213

Visit Hal Leonard Online at
www.halleonard.com

CARPENTERS

BLESS THE BEASTS AND CHILDREN

Words and Music by BARRY DeVORZON
and PERRY BOTKIN, JR.

Fm/A♭ G7♯5 Cm
chil - dren, for the world can nev - er be
Fsus F B♭ Gsus G
the world they see.
E♭ E♭maj7 D♭/E♭
mf
Light their way when the dark - ness sur -
Fm/E♭ E♭ F C♭/G♭ G♭
rounds them; Give them love let it

D♭/F
E♭/F
F
shine all a - round them.
B♭
Fm/A♭
G7
mp
Bless the beasts and the chil - dren;
Give them shel - ter
Cm
Fsus
F
B♭
from a storm;
Keep them safe;
Gsus
G
C
8va
Keep them warm.
rit.
p

(They Long to Be)
CLOSE TO YOU

Lyric by HAL DAVID
Music by BURT BACHARACH

Slowly with a steady beat

Fmaj7
C6
Cmaj7
Just like me they long to be close to you.
C6
C7
F
On the day that you were born the an-gels got to-geth-er and de-
mf
Em7
A7
F
cid-ed to cre-ate a dream come true. So, they sprink-led moon dust in your hair of
G
N.C.
gold and star-light in your eyes of blue. That is
rall.
mp

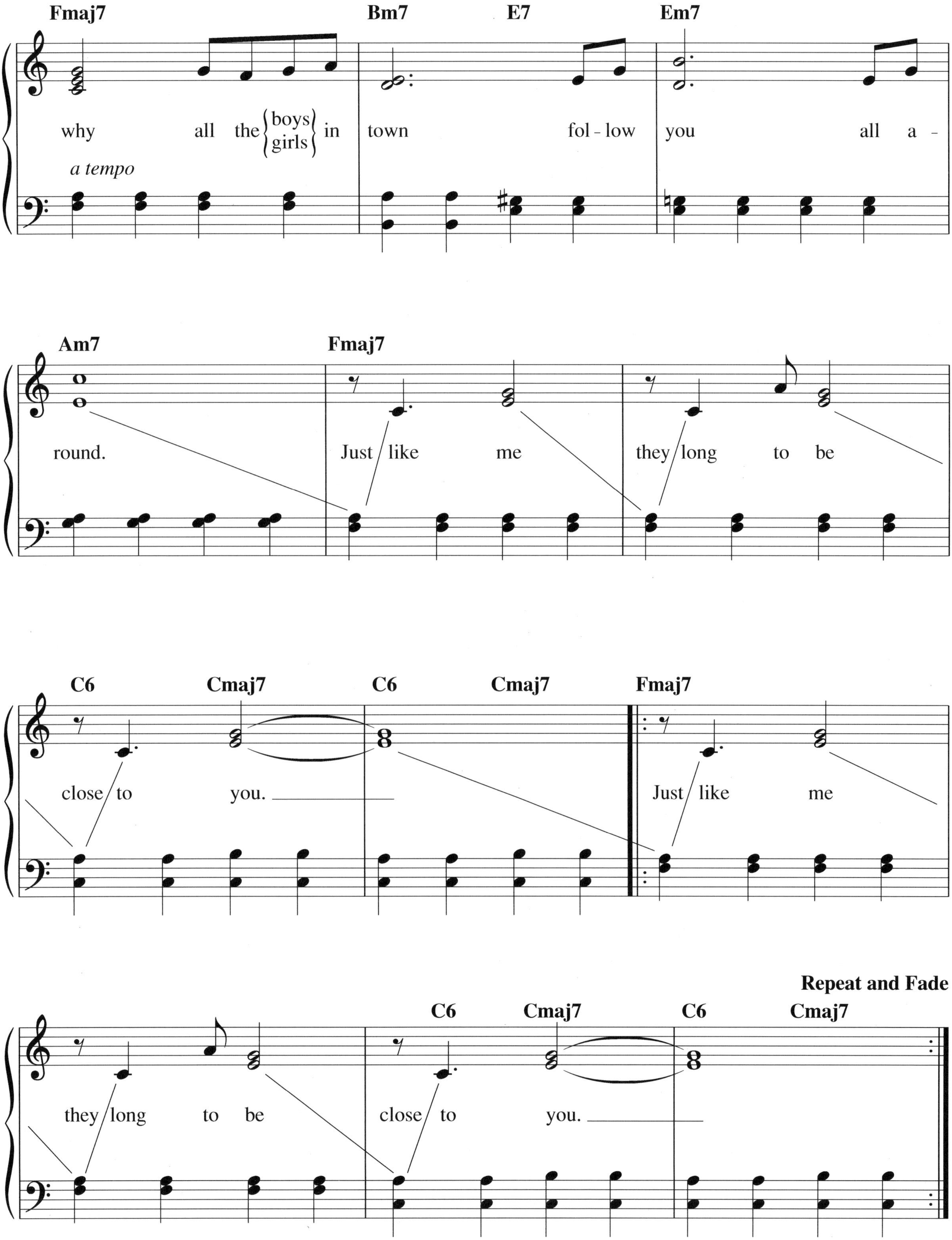
Fmaj7
Bm7
E7
Em7
why all the boys / girls in town fol - low you all a -
a tempo
Am7
Fmaj7
round. Just like me they long to be
C6
Cmaj7
C6
Cmaj7
Fmaj7
close to you.
Just like me
Repeat and Fade
C6
Cmaj7
C6
Cmaj7
they long to be close to you.

FOR ALL WE KNOW

from the Motion Picture LOVERS AND OTHER STRANGERS

Words by ROBB WILSON and JAMES GRIFFIN
Music by FRED KARLIN

Not too slow - very steady

G Cmaj7 F B♭maj7
So much to say, And as we go
Gm7 Gm7/C F G/B
Melody
from day to day I'll feel you close to me,
Gm/B♭ F/A
But time a - lone will tell.
F C/E Dm Dm/C G7/B
Let's take a life - time to say,

G7
Cmaj7
F
B♭maj7
"I knew you well."
For on - ly time
Gm
C
C/B♭
Am7
Dm7
B♭maj7
will tell us so,
And love may grow for
Gm7/C
F
C addF
all we know.
p
B♭/C
C7sus
Gm11
Fmaj9
pp
8va lower

GOODBYE TO LOVE

Words and Music by RICHARD CARPENTER
and JOHN BETTIS

Slowly, with expression

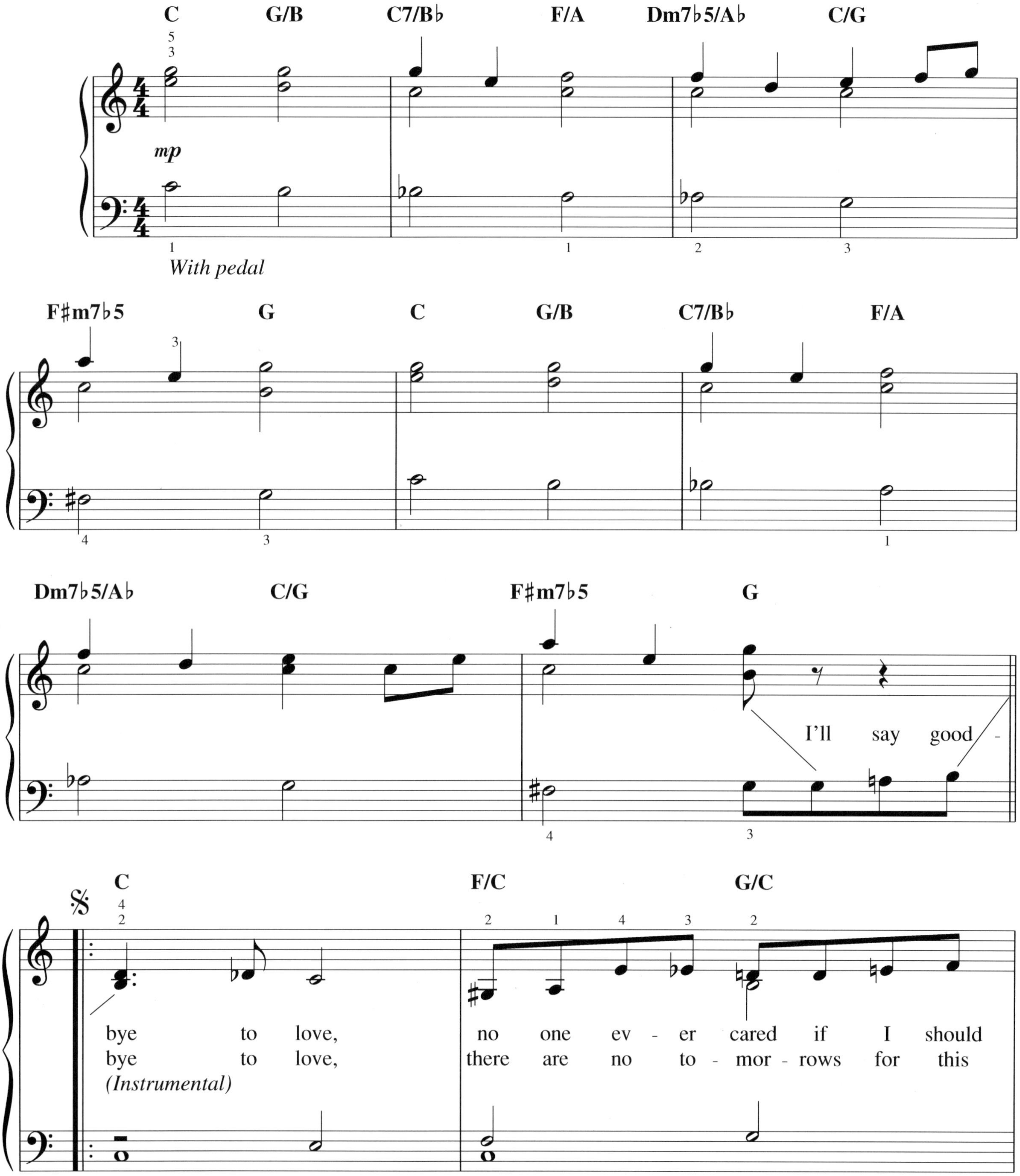

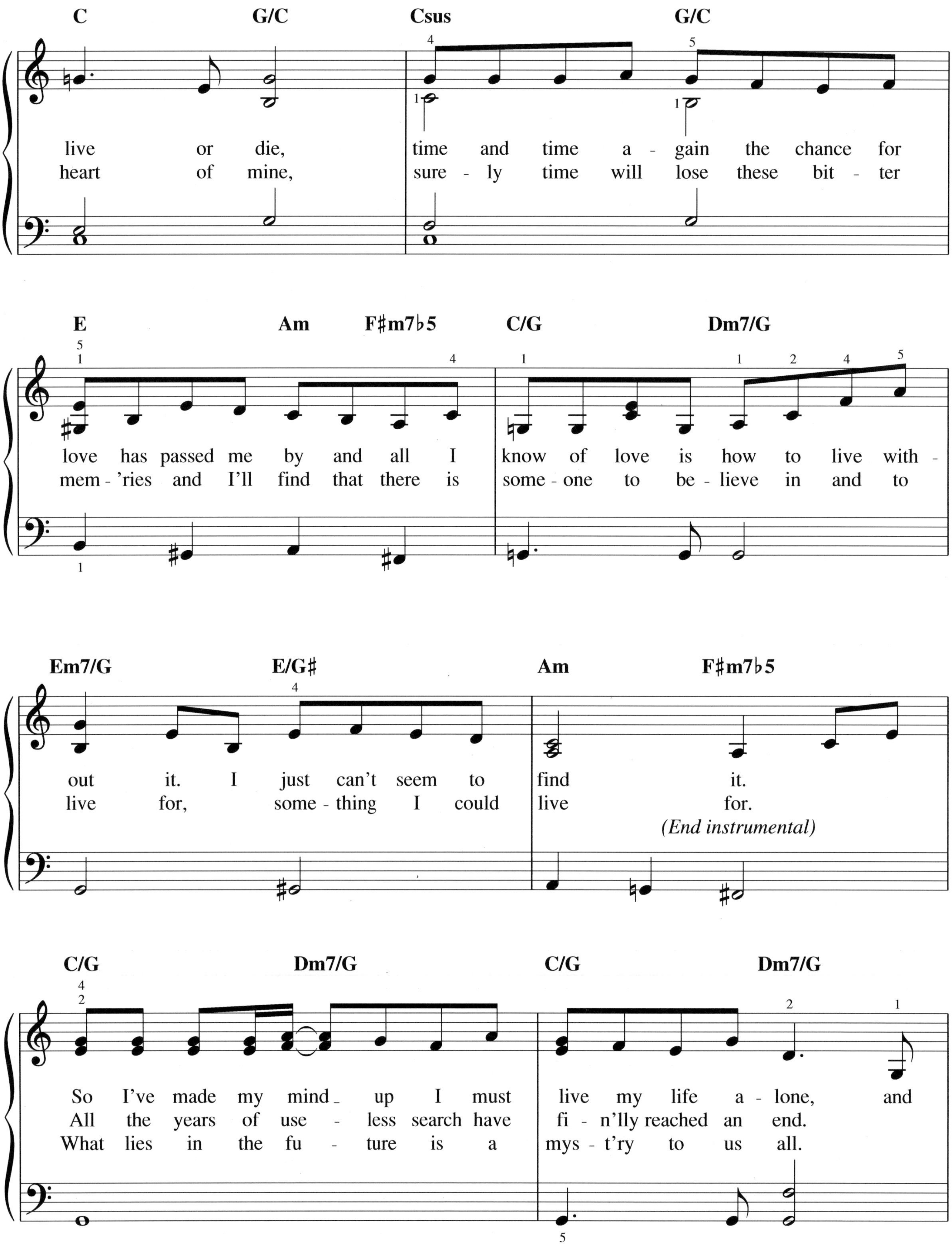
C G/C Csus G/C
live or die, time and time a - gain the chance for
heart of mine, sure - ly time will lose these bit - ter
E Am F♯m7♭5 C/G Dm7/G
love has passed me by and all I know of love is how to live with -
mem - 'ries and I'll find that there is some - one to be - lieve in and to
Em7/G E/G♯ Am F♯m7♭5
out it. I just can't seem to find it.
live for, some - thing I could live for.
(End instrumental)
C/G Dm7/G C/G Dm7/G
So I've made my mind up I must live my life a - lone, and
All the years of use - less search have fi - n'lly reached an end.
What lies in the fu - ture is a mys - t'ry to us all.

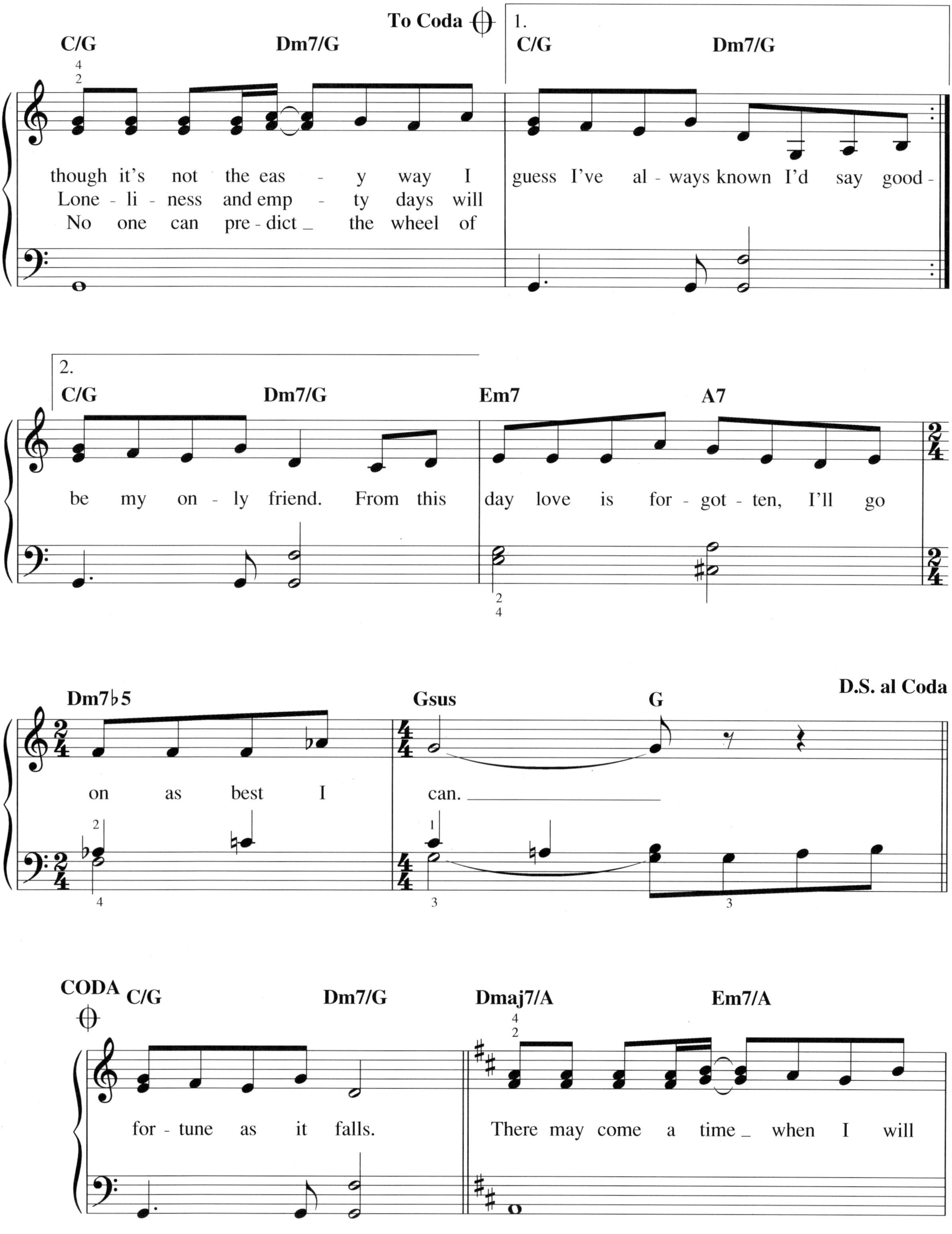
To Coda
1.
C/G
Dm7/G
though it's not the eas - y way I
Lone - li - ness and emp - ty days will
No one can pre - dict the wheel of
guess I've al - ways known I'd say good -
2.
Em7
A7
be my on - ly friend. From this
day love is for - got - ten, I'll go
Dm7♭5
Gsus
G
D.S. al Coda
on as best I
can.
CODA
Dmaj7/A
Em7/A
for - tune as it falls.
There may come a time when I will

Dmaj7/A
Em7/A
Dmaj7
see that I've been wrong. But for
now this is my
Em7
A7
D
song. ___ And it's good - bye to love.
G/A
D
I'll say good - bye to love.
G/A
D
A/C♯

D7/C
G/B
Em7♭5/B♭
D/A
G♯m7♭5
A
1
D
A/C♯
D7/C
G/B
Em7♭5/B♭
D/A
G♯m7♭5
A
D
G/A
D
G/A
D(add9)

HURTING EACH OTHER

Words by PETER UDELL
Music by GARY GELD

Fm7
Ab/Bb
Cmaj9
love I give glad - ly to you, all your love you give
life I could love on - ly you, all your life you could
D/C
Fmaj7
C/E
Dm7
Dm7/G
glad - ly to me. Tell me why then, oh why should it be that
love on - ly me. Tell me why then, oh why should it be that
C
Dm7/C
C
we go on hurt - ing each oth - er! We go on
Dm7/C
C
Dm7/C
C
hurt - ing each oth - er! Mak - ing each oth - er cry, hurt - ing each oth - er with -

B♭/C
F/C
C
out ev - er know - ing
why.
1.
2.
C
Dm7/C
Can't we stop
hurt-ing each oth - er!
C
Dm7/C
C
Got - ta stop
hurt - ing each oth - er!
Mak - ing each oth - er cry.
Repeat and Fade
Dm7/C
C
Dm7/C
C
B♭
G7
Break - ing each oth - er's heart.
Tear - ing each oth - er a -
part.

ONLY YESTERDAY

Words and Music by RICHARD CARPENTER
and JOHN BETTIS

Moderate Rock (2 beat feel)

To Coda
A7/C♯
D
G/B
time no - bod - y knew the pain I was go - in'
us, share it with me, the best is a - bout to
C
Am7
D7sus
thru, and wait - in' was all my heart could do.
D7
G
Hope was all I had un - til you
A7/G
F♯dim
came, may - be you can't

G
see how much you mean to me.
Em
A7/C♯
D
You were the dawn break-ing the night, the
G/B
C
A7/C♯
prom-ise of morn-ing light, fill-ing the world sur-
D7
F
round-ing me. When I hold you, ba-by, ba-by,

Am
feels like may - be things will be ___ all right.
F
F/E♭
Dsus
Ba - by, ba - by, your love's made ___ me free as a song, ___
D7
G
sing - in' for - ev - er. On - ly yes - ter - day ___ when I was
Am7
D7
G
sad and I was lone - ly you showed me the way

Am7
D7
— to leave the past and all its tears be - hind — me.
B7
Em
To - mor - row may be e - ven bright - er than — to -
E7sus
E7
Am7
D7
day since I threw — my sad - ness — a -
Am7/G
G
way. On - ly yes - ter - day. —

D.S. al Coda
Am7/G
CODA
C
A7/G
D7
be. And
so much is left for
us to see.
When I hold you,
F
ba - by, ba - by,
feels like may - be
Am
things will be all
right.
F
Ba - by, ba - by,

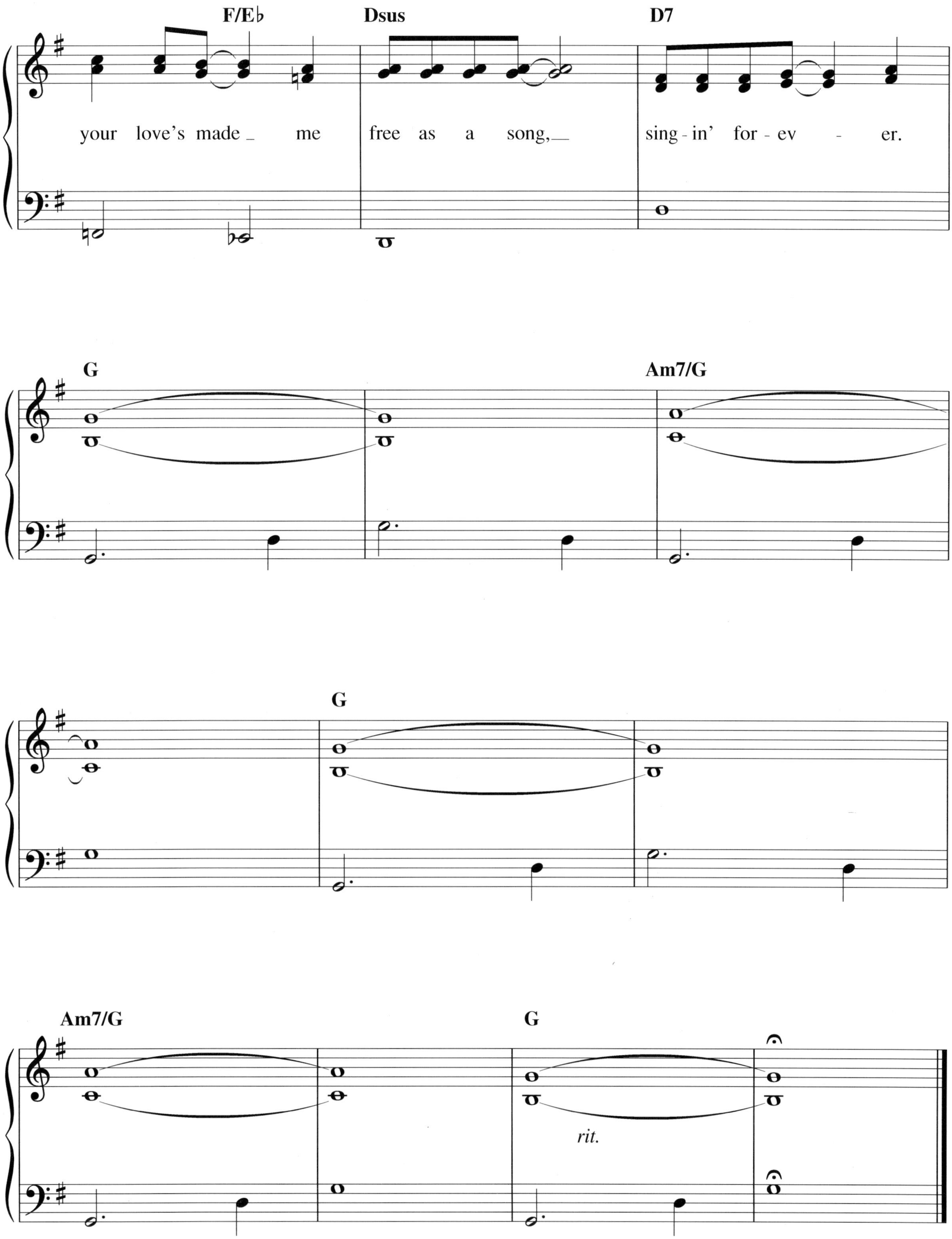
F/E♭
Dsus
D7
your love's made me free as a song, sing-in' for-ev-er.
G
Am7/G
G
Am7/G
G
rit.

I WON'T LAST A DAY WITHOUT YOU

Words and Music by PAUL WILLIAMS
and ROGER NICHOLS

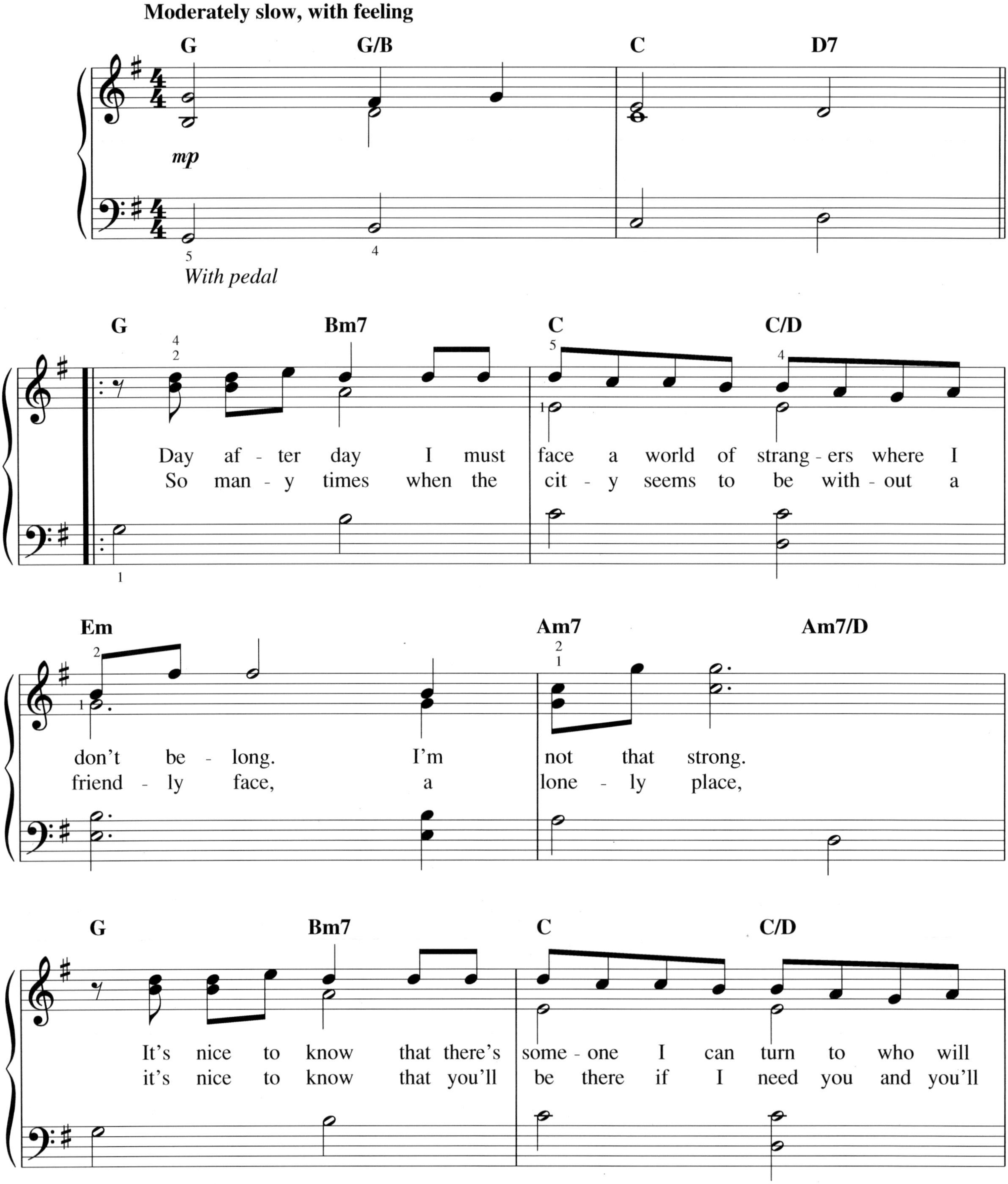

Em
Am7
Am7/D
al - ways care, you're al - ways there.
al - ways smile, it's all worth - while.
When there's
G
G/B
C(add9)
Am7
Am7/D
no get - ting o - ver that rain - bow, when my
G
G/B
C
Am7
Am7/D
small - est of dreams won't come true, I can
G
F/G
Cmaj7
G/B
take all the mad - ness the world has to give, but I

1.
Am7 D7 G G/B C D7
won't last a day with - out you.
2.
G G(add9) Em7 A7 Dmaj7
you. Touch me and I end up sing - ing,
Em7 A7 B7sus B7
trou - bles seem to up and dis - ap - pear, you
C♯m7 F♯7 Bmaj7
touch me with the love you're bring - ing,

G♯m7 Amaj7 B7sus B7
I can't real - ly lose when you're near. When you're
Am7 D7 G Bm7
near my ___ love, if all my friends have for -
C C/D Em
got - ten half their prom - is - es they're not un - kind, just
Am7 C/D G Bm7
hard to find. One look at you and I

C C/D Em
know that I could learn to live with - out the rest, I
Am7 Am7/D G G/B
found the best. When there's no get - ting o - ver that
C(add9) Am7 Am7/D G G/B
rain - bow, when my small - est of dreams won't come
C Am7 Am7/D G F/G
true, I can take all the mad - ness the

1.
Cmaj7 G/B Am7 D7
world __ has to give, but I won't last a day with - out
G Am7/D
you. When there's
2.
Am7 D7sus D7
won't last a day ____ with - out
G G/B C D7 G G/B
you.
C D7 G(add9)

IT'S GOING TO TAKE SOME TIME

Words and Music by CAROLE KING
and TONI STERN

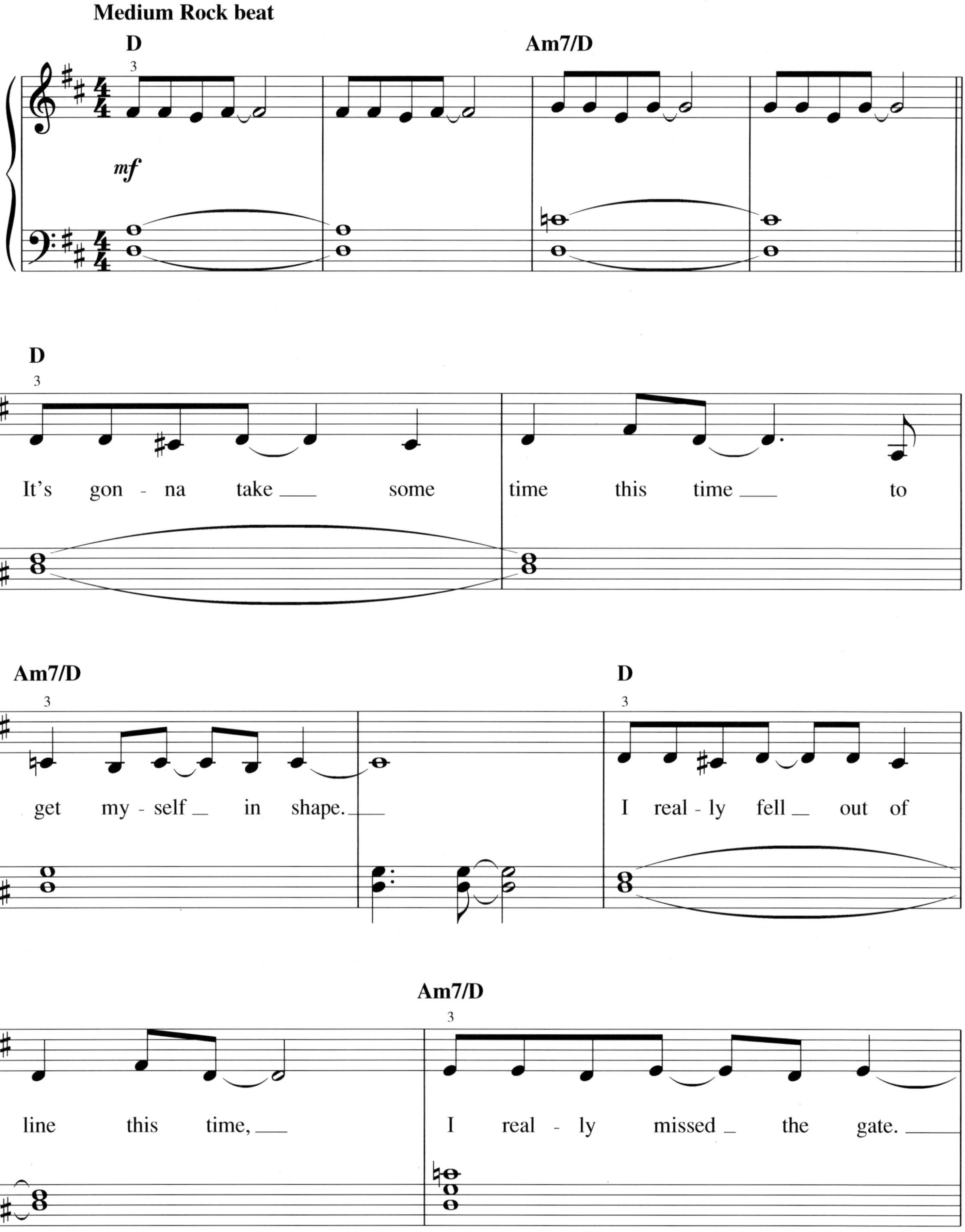

Gmaj7
F♯m7
The birds on the tel - e - phone line, (next time) are
Gmaj7
F♯m7
Gmaj7
cry - in' out to me, (next time) and I won't be so
F♯m7
Bm7
Em7
A7sus
blind next time, and I'll find some har - mo - ny. But, it's
D
go - ing to take some time this time, and
go - ing to take some time this time, no

Am7/D
I can't make de - mands. But, like the
mat - ter what I've planned. And, like the
D
Am7/D
young trees in the win - ter time, I'll learn how to bend.
Gmaj7
F♯m7
Af - ter all the tears we've spent, how
Em7
A7
D
Bm
Bm/A♯
could we make a - mends? So, it's one more round for ex -

Bm/A
Bm/G♯
G/A
Em/A
pe - ri - ence and I'm on the road _ a - gain, and it's
Gmaj9
F♯m7
Em7
Em7/A
1.
D
go - ing to take _ some time this ___ time. ___
But, it's
2.
D
time. ___
Am7/D
D(add9)

MERRY CHRISTMAS, DARLING

Words and Music by RICHARD CARPENTER
and FRANK POOLER

Dm/C Cmaj7 Am7 Gm7 C7
dar - ling. We're a - part that's true; but
F G/F Em7 Am7 Dm7 Em
I can dream and in my dreams, I'm Christ - mas - ing with
F6 G Cmaj7 Dm/C
you. Hol - i - days are joy - ful,
Cmaj7 Gm7 C7 F G/F
there's al - ways some - thing new. But ev - 'ry day's a

Em7 Am7 D/F♯ Fm6 B♭9
hol - i - day when I'm near to you. The
E♭ F/E♭ Dm7 Gm Cm7 F7
lights on my tree I wish you could see, I wish it ev - 'ry
B♭ Gm Gm(maj7) Gm7 Dm7 G7
day. The logs on the fire fill me with de - sire
Cmaj7 Dm7 Em7 Am7 Dm7 G7
to see you and to say that I

Cmaj7 Dm/C Cmaj7
wish you mer - ry Christ - mas, hap - py New Year
Gm7 C7 F G/F Em7 Am7
too. I've just one wish on this Christ-mas Eve;
1. 2.
Dm7 G7 C B♭9 Dm7 G7
I wish I were with you. The I wish I were with
Em7♭5 A7 Dm7 G7 N.C. B♭ C
you. I wish I were with you.
rit.

PLEASE MR. POSTMAN

Words and Music by ROBERT BATEMAN,
GEORGIA DOBBINS, WILLIAM GARRETT,
FREDDIE GORMAN and BRIAN HOLLAND

C
3
Am
There must be some word to - day
from my boy - friend
F
so far a - way,
please, Mis - ter Post - man,
look and see
G
5
1
C
if there's a let - ter, a let - ter for me.
I've been stand - ing here
Am
3
F
1
wait - ing, Mis - ter Post - man,
so
pa - tient - ly,
for just a card

G
or just a let - ter,
say - ing he's re - turn - ing
home to me. Mis - ter
C
Am
Post - man,
look and see
if there's a let - ter in your
bag for me,
F
G
3
1
why's it tak - ing
such a long time
for me to hear from that
C
Am
boy of mine?
(Instrumental)

F
G
C
Am
So man - y days you passed me by, see the tears stand-ing
F
G
in my eyes, you did-n't stop to make me feel bet - ter, by leav-ing me a
C
card or a let - ter. Mis - ter Post - man, look and see

Am
if there's a let - ter in your bag for me,
F
why's it tak - ing
such a long time, why don't you
G
check it and see one more
time for me? You got to
C
wait a min-ute, wait a min-ute,
Am
wait a min-ute, wait a min-ute,
F
Mis - ter Post - man,

G
look and see, come on de - liv - er the let - ter, the soon - er the bet - ter.
C
Am
(Instrumental)
F
G
1.
2.
C

RAINY DAYS AND MONDAYS

Lyrics by PAUL WILLIAMS
Music by ROGER NICHOLS

Em7 Cmaj7 Am7 C/D G
Hang - in' a - round noth - ing to do but frown;
Walk - in' a - round some kind of lone - ly clown;
Hang - in' a - round noth - ing to do but frown;
Am7 C/D G/D D7sus
rain-y days and Mon-days al - ways get me down.
1.
G/D D7sus
2.,3.
G/D B/D♯ Em7 Cmaj7 Am7 D7 Gmaj7
Fun - ny but it seems I al - ways wind up here with you,
Bm7 Cmaj7 C/D D B7/D♯
nice to know some-bod - y loves me.

Em7 Cmaj7 Am7 D7 Bm
Fun - ny but it seems that it's the on - ly thing I do,
To Coda
D.S. al Coda
Bm7 Cmaj7 D7sus D7 Am7
run and find the one who loves _ me.
CODA
Dm7 G7 C Em/B Em7♭5 A7
What I feel has come and gone be - fore,
Dm11 Em7 Fmaj7 Em7
no need to talk it out,
we know what it's all a - bout.

Am7
Fmaj7
Dm7
F/G
C
Hang - in' a - round noth - in' to do but frown;
1.
Dm7
F/G
C/G
E/G♯
rain - y days and Mon - days al - ways get me down.
2.
Dm7
F/G
C/G
rain - y days and Mon - days al - ways get me down.
G7sus
C/G
G7sus
Cmaj7

SING

Words and Music by
JOE RAPOSO

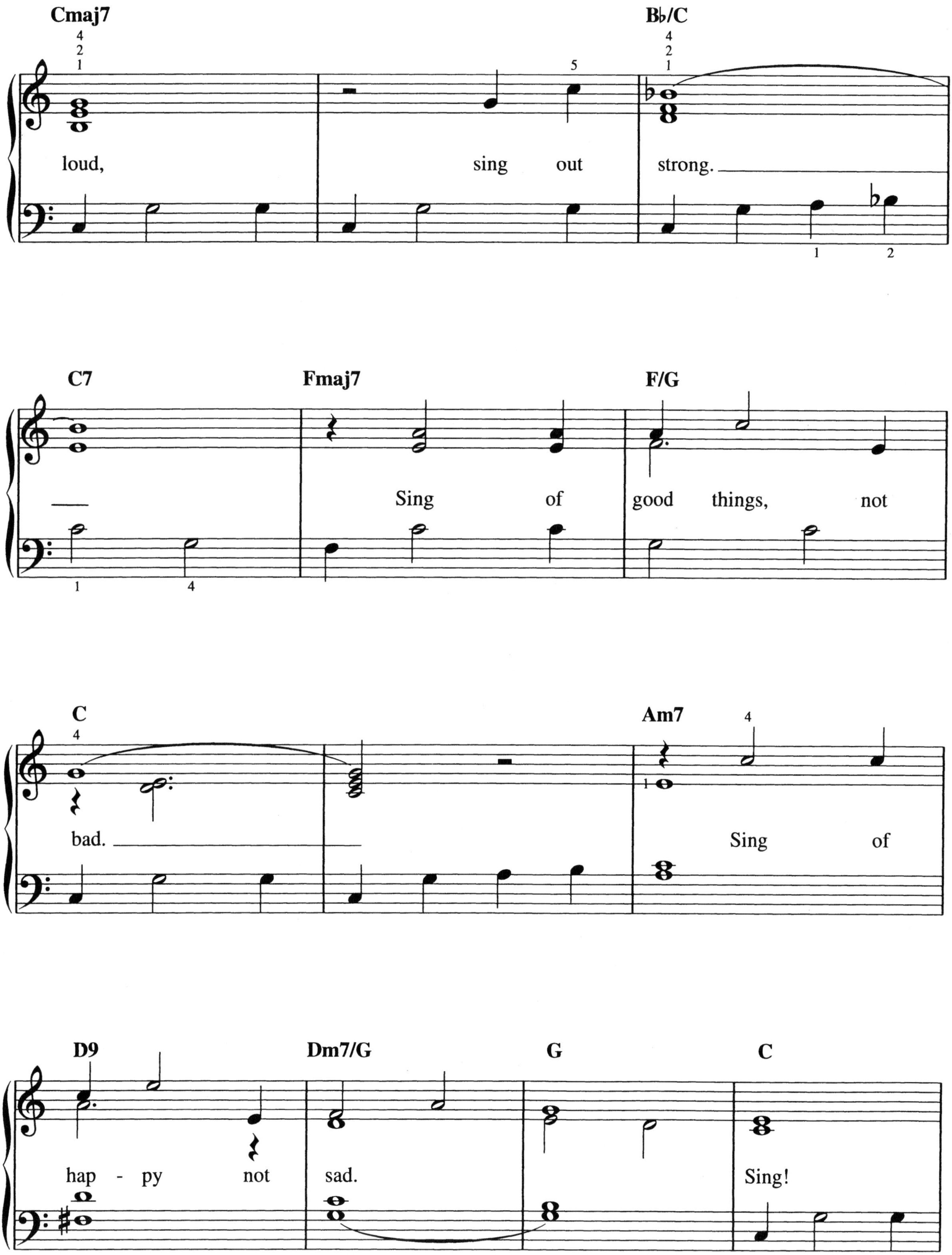
Cmaj7
B♭/C
loud, sing out strong.
C7
Fmaj7
F/G
Sing of good things, not
C
Am7
bad.
Sing of
D9
Dm7/G
G
C
hap - py not sad.
Sing!

Dm7/C
C
Sing a song. Make it simple to
Cmaj7
C6
Gm7/C
C9
last your whole life long. Don't
Fmaj7
E+
Am7
worry that it's not good enough for anyone else to
D9
G7sus
G7
C
hear. Sing! Sing a song.

La la do la da, la
Cmaj7
Fmaj7
F/G
da la do la da, la
da da la do la
da.
C
Cmaj7
La la do la da, la
da la do la da, la
1.
2.
Fmaj7
F/G
F/G
C
da da la do la
da.
da.

SOLITAIRE

Words and Music by NEIL SEDAKA
and PHIL CODY

Slowly, with Expression

G7 C
un - til it died with - in his si - lence.
who would com- mand the hand he's play - ing.
G7 sus G7 C
And sol - i - taire's the on - ly game in town, and
mf
Am
ev - 'ry road that takes him takes him down. And
Dm7 G7
by him - self it's eas - y to pre - tend he'll nev - er

F/C C Dm7 G7 C
love a - gain. And keep - ing to him - self he plays the
Am
game; with- out her love it al - ways ends the same. While
Dm7 1 G7 F/C C
life goes on a - round him ev - 'ry - where, he's play - ing sol - i - taire.
F G 2 G7 C
where, he's play - ing sol - i - taire.

TOP OF THE WORLD

Words and Music by JOHN BETTIS
and RICHARD CARPENTER

D
G
see, not a cloud in the
same, in the leaves on the
A
F♯m7
B7
sky got the sun in my eyes, and I
trees and the touch of the breeze, there's a
Em7
Em7♭5
Asus
won't be sur - prised if it's a dream.
pleas - in' sense of hap - pi - ness for me.
A
D
A
G
Ev - 'ry - thing I want the world to
There is on - ly one wish on my

D
F♯m
be, is now com - ing true es -
mind, when this day is through I
Em7
A7
D
pe - cial - ly for me, and the
hope that I will find, that to -
G
A
F♯m7
rea - son is clear, it's be - cause you are
mor - row will be just the same for you and
B7
Em7
Em7♭5
here, you're the near - est thing to heav - en that I've
me, all I need will be mine if you are

Asus
A
D
seen.
here.
I'm on the top of the world
look - in'
G
down on cre - a - tion and the
D
Em7
A7
D
on - ly ex - pla - na - tion I can find,
G
A
is the love that I've found, ev - er

D G D
since you've been a - round, your love's put me at the
Em A7 D G D G
3
1
top of the world.
1.
D G D N.C.
2.
D G D

SUPERSTAR

Words and Music by LEON RUSSELL
and BONNIE SHERIDAN

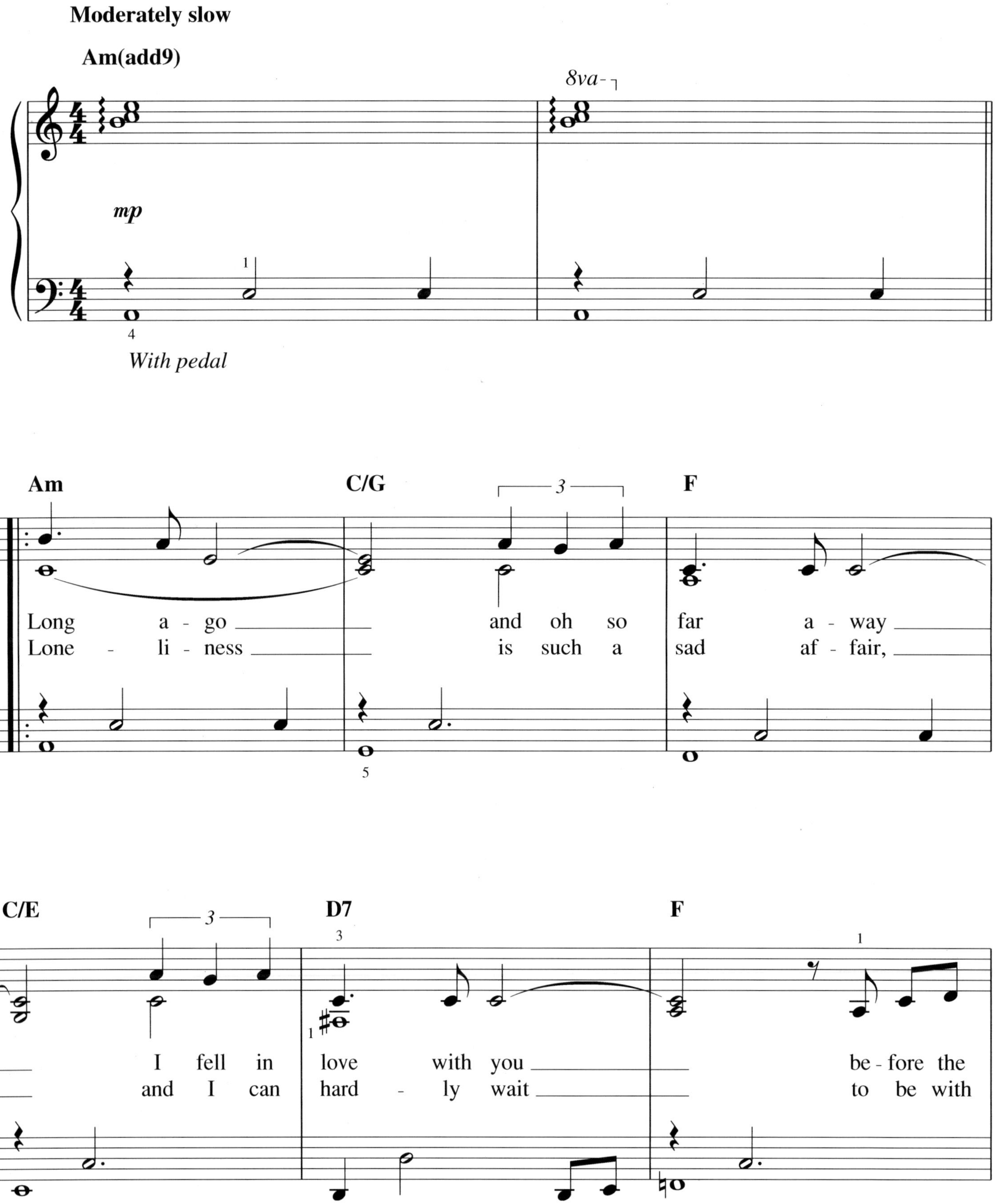

Em7
E7
Am
sec - ond show.
you a - gain.
Your gui - tar
What to say
C/G
F
C/E
it sounds so sweet and clear,
but you're not
to make you come a - gain,
come back to
D7
F
Em
real - ly here,
it's just the ra - di - o.
me a - gain
and play your sad gui - tar.
E7
F
Em
Dm
Don't you re - mem - ber you told me you loved me,

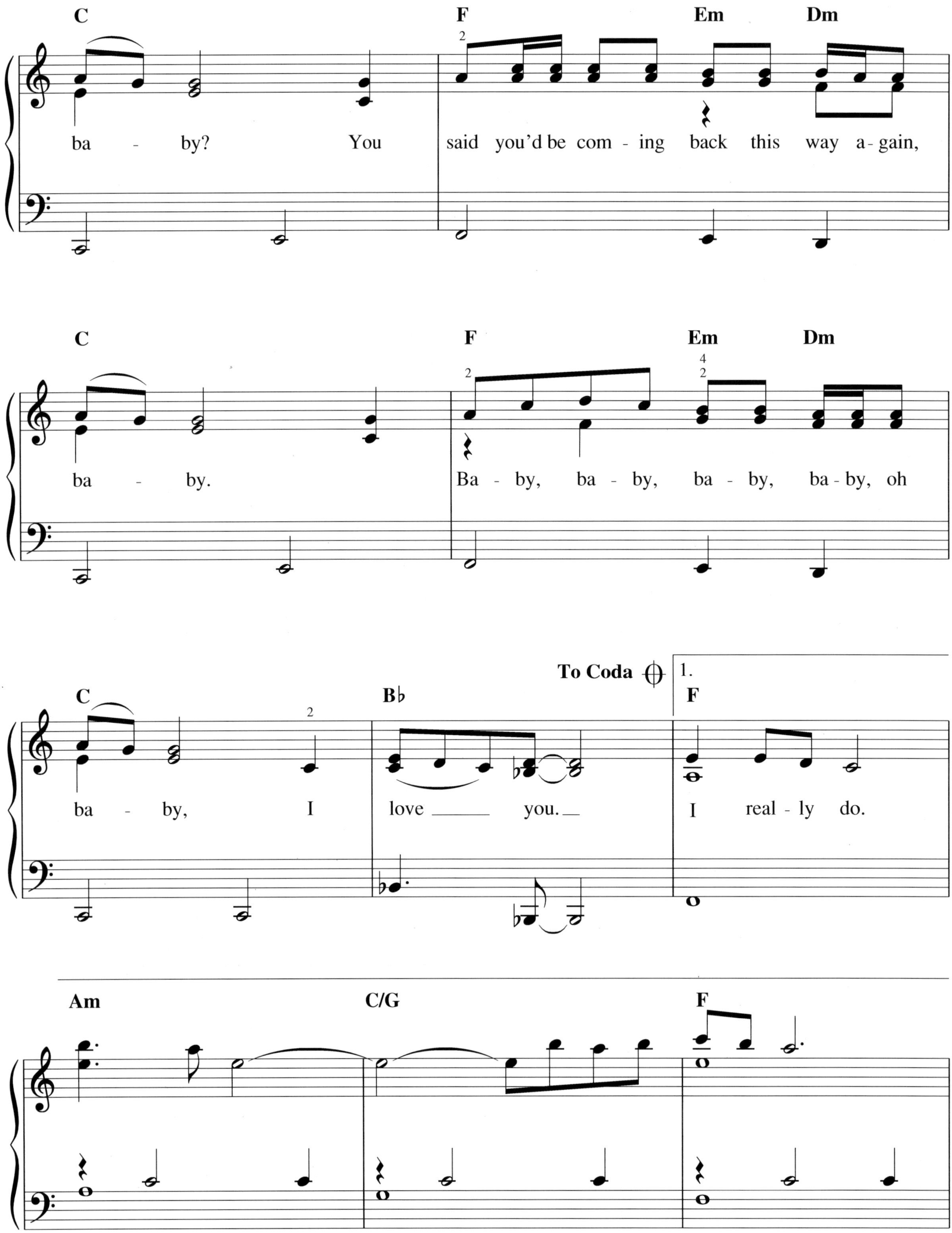
C
F
Em
Dm
ba - by? You
said you'd be com - ing back this way a - gain,
C
F
Em
Dm
ba - by.
Ba - by, ba - by, ba - by, ba - by, oh
To Coda
1.
C
B♭
F
ba - by, I
love you.
I real - ly do.
Am
C/G
F

C/E
D7
G
F/G
Em7
Am(add9)
8va
2.
F
E7
D.S. al Coda
I real - ly do.
CODA
F
8va
Am(add9)
I real - ly do.
rit.
p
8vb

THERE'S A KIND OF HUSH
(All Over the World)

Words and Music by LES REED
and GEOFF STEPHENS

G
B7
Em
2
two of us and no - bod - y else in
G7
C
2
sight. There's no - bod - y else and I'm feel - ing
D7
G
good just hold - ing you tight.
G7
C
4
2
2
1
So lis - ten ver - y

C6
Cmaj7
C6
care - ful - ly, ___
clos - er now and
you will see what I
G
mean.
It is - n't a
dream.
G7
C
C6
The
on - ly sound that
you will hear is
Cmaj7
C6
D7
when I whis - per
in your ear, "I love
you

for - ev - er and ev - er." There's a
G
kind of hush
B7
all o - ver the
Em
world to -
G7
night, all o - ver the
C
world you can hear the
D7
sounds of lov - ers in
G
love.

WE'VE ONLY JUST BEGUN

Words and Music by ROGER NICHOLS
and PAUL WILLIAMS

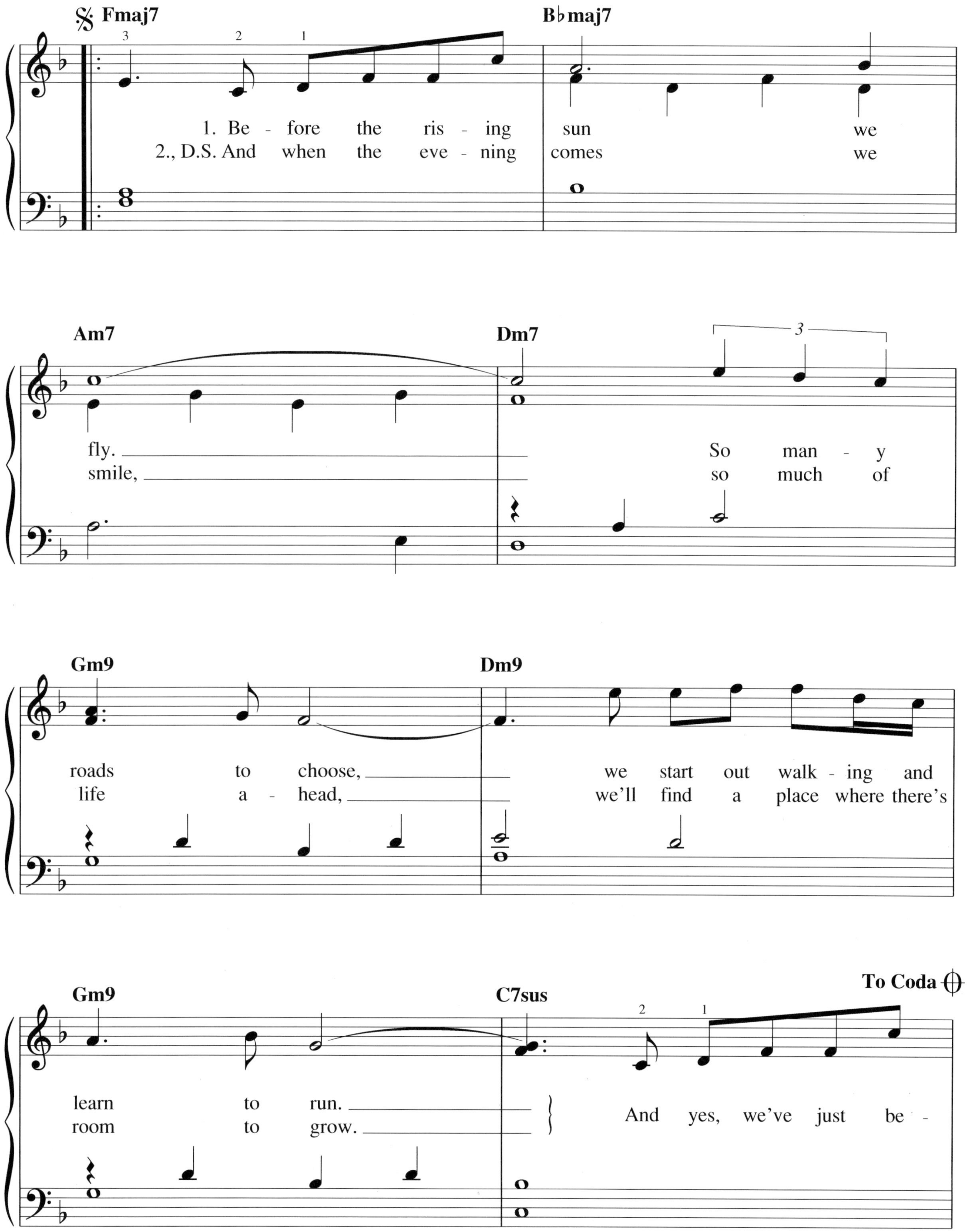
Fmaj7
B♭maj7
1. Be - fore the ris - ing sun we
2., D.S. And when the eve - ning comes we
Am7
Dm7
fly. So man - y
smile, so much of
Gm9
Dm9
roads to choose, we start out walk - ing and
life a - head, we'll find a place where there's
Gm9
C7sus
To Coda
learn to run.
room to grow.
And yes, we've just be -

Fmaj7 B♭maj7 Fmaj7 B♭maj7 C
gun.
D Gmaj7 D Gmaj7
Shar - ing hor - i - zons that are new to us,
D Gmaj7 D Gmaj7
watch - ing the signs a - long the way.
G♭ C♭maj7 G♭ C♭maj7
Talk - ing it o - ver just the two of us,

G♭
C♭maj7
C7sus
work - ing to - geth - er day to day, to -
1.
C9sus
geth - er.
2.
C9sus
geth - er, to -
C7sus
geth - er.
D.S. al Coda
CODA
F(add9)
B♭(add9)
F(add9)
gun.
B♭(add9)
A
rit.

YESTERDAY ONCE MORE

Words and Music by JOHN BETTIS
and RICHARD CARPENTER

D
F♯m/C♯
hap - py times and not so long a - go how I
songs of love that I would sing to then and I'd
Bm
Bm/A
Gmaj7
C♯m7♭5
F♯7
won - dered where they'd gone but they're
mem - o - rize each word. Those old
Bm
Bm/A
back a - gain just like a long lost friend all the
mel - o - dies still sound so good to me as they
Gmaj7
Em7
G/A
A7
songs I love so well.
melt the years a - way.
Ev - 'ry

D
Bm
sha - la - la - la ev - 'ry wo wo still
D
Bm7
shines. Ev - 'ry
D
Bm
shing - a - ling - a - ling that they're start - in' to sing so
Em7
A7
fine.
When they
All my

Bm
get to the part where he's
best mem - o - ries come back
B♭+
break - ing her heart it can
clear - ly to me some can
D/A
real - ly make me
e - ven make me
G♯m7♭5
cry just like be -
cry just like be -
D/A
fore.
fore.
G/A
It's yes - ter - day once
Dmaj7
more.
1.
G/A
Dmaj7
G/A
Look - in'
2.
G/A
A7
Ev - 'ry

D
Bm
D
sha - la - la - la ___ ev - 'ry wo __ wo _____ still shines.
Bm7
D
Ev - 'ry shing - a - ling - a - ling that they're
Bm7
Em7
1.
A7
G/A
A7
start - in' to sing __ so fine. Ev - 'ry
2.
A7
G/A
Dmaj7